Little Book of Answers

Who Is This?

Written by Michele Ashley

Families

Vital Vocabulary

brother   8

family   14

father 6

me 12

mother 4

sister 10

This is my mother.

This is my father.

This is my brother.

This is my sister.

This is me.

This is my family.

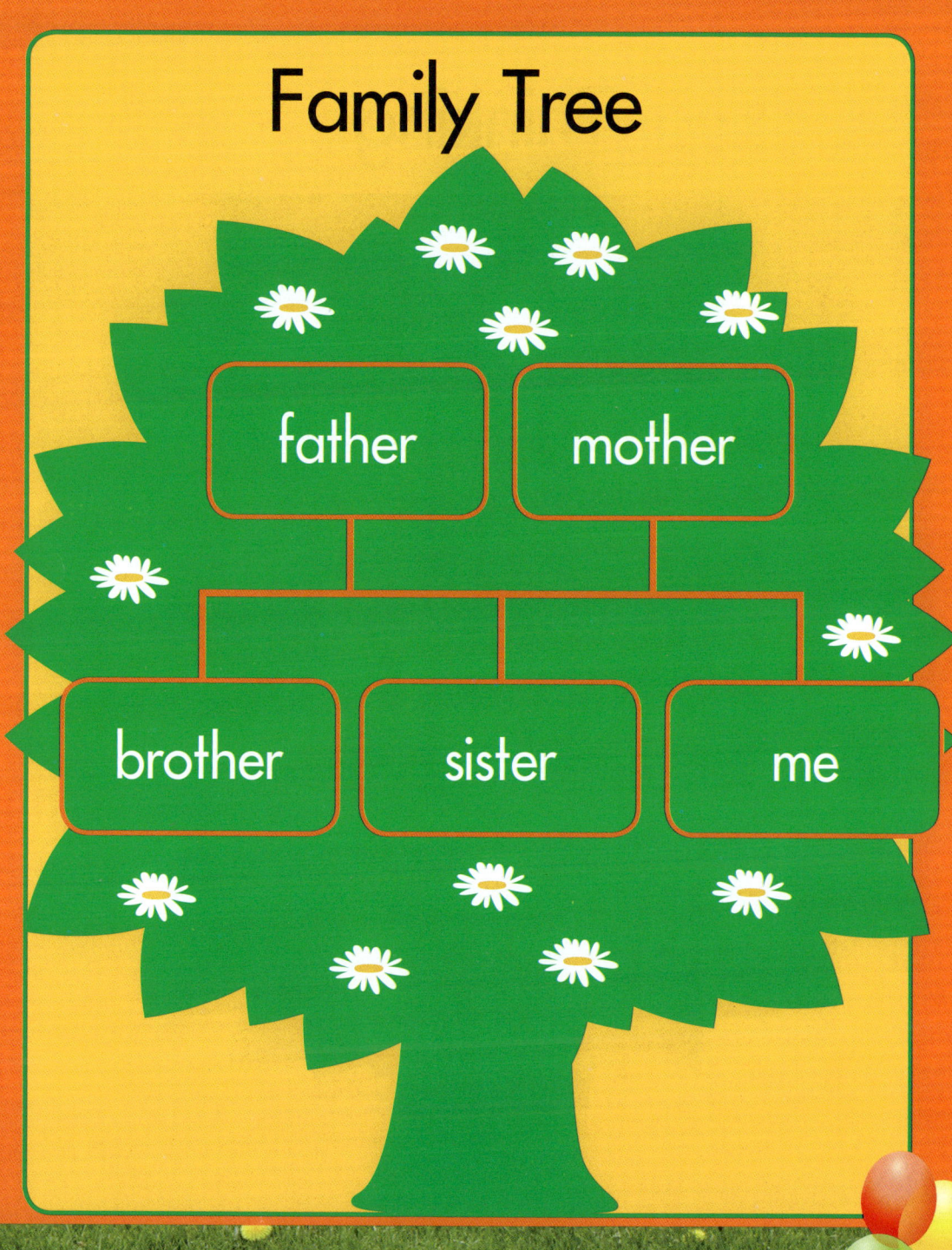

Critical Thinking

Draw a family tree like this with your family in it.